Solitude Is Company, Love Is a Crowd

Andre D. Woods

4S1

SOLITUDE IS COMPANY, LOVE IS A CROWD
WRITTEN AND ARRANGED BY **ANDRE D. WOODS**
ALL RIGHTS RESERVED.

NO PART OF THIS PUBLICATION MAY BE REPRODUCED, DISTRIBUTED, OR TRANSMITTED IN ANY FORM OR BY ANY MEANS, INCLUDING PHOTOCOPYING, RECORDING, OR OTHER ELECTRONIC OR MECHANICAL METHODS, WITHOUT THE PRIOR WRITTEN PERMISSION OF THE PUBLISHER, EXCEPT IN BRIEF QUOTATIONS EMBODIED IN CRITICAL REVIEWS, CITATIONS, AND LITERARY JOURNALS FOR NONCOMMERCIAL USES PERMITTED BY COPYRIGHT LAW. FOR PERMISSION REQUESTS, EMAIL US AT LEGAL@UNDERWATERMOUNTAINS.BIZ
WITH THE BODY: "ATTENTION: PERMISSIONS COORDINATOR

COVER ART AND DESIGN BY
MITCH GREEN

COPYRIGHT 2015 © 451 PRESS
WWW.451.PRESS

This book is for the Lonely

This book is for the Lovers

This book is for the Wounded

This book is for the Scarred

This book is for Solitude

Contents

Foreword	9
P H A S E 1 : *A Loan*	15
A Loan:	17
Moon Lovers:	18
Rain Drops:	19
Liquor Infused:	21
Party Girl:	22
Gone Genius:	23
Eyes Tell Lies:	24
Morning Ritual:	26
Body of Time:	28
Band-Aid Boy:	29
Love Sick:	30
Losing It:	32
All in a Night's Work:	33
Cheers to You:	34
Rose:	36
Soul Switch:	38
Stood a Chance:	39
Dreamless Evenings:	40
Pretty Big City:	41
Cold Summer:	42
"Average Joe" – Words from Jane:	44
"Average Jane" – Words from Joe:	45
The Feels:	46
Yesterday's Junky:	47
Talking to Myself:	48
Post-traumatic love:	49

PHASE 2: *Love: Oblivion at Its Finest* — 51

- Love: Oblivion at Its Finest — 53
- The Greats: — 55
- Nourishing Pain: — 56
- Been There Done That: — 57
- Unreal: — 58
- Best of Both Worlds: — 59
- A Love/Fear Poem: — 60
- Fun and Games: — 61
- Instincts: — 62
- A Great Fuck: — 63
- Filthy Gentlemen: — 64
- All But Slow: — 67
- Midnight: — 68
- Universal Attraction: — 69
- Fuck Buddies: — 70
- Staring Problem: — 71
- Layers: — 73
- Toast: — 74

PHASE 3: *Crowded by Love* — 77

- Crowded by Love: — 79
- Business Is Booming: — 80
- Twisted Attraction: — 81
- Smokers and Lovers: — 82
- Houdini: — 83
- Half Empty Is Enough: — 84
- Shadow: — 85
- Mind Within Matter: — 86
- Simply Complex: — 87

Good Gal:	88
Out of Mind:	89
Smart Phones, Dumb Love:	90
World vs. I:	91
The Getaway:	93

PHASE 4 : *Accompanied by Solitude*   95

Accompanied by Solitude:	97
Tattoos and I:	99
Forget:	100
Disappear:	101
Break the Heart:	102
Safe in Pain:	103
Bars and Dreams:	104
Writer's Ink:	105
Coffee Shops:	106
Shhhh:	107
Company:	109
Mr. Know It All:	110
Laws:	112
Voids:	113
Another Day, Another Drive:	114
Perspective:	116
Non-Social Media:	117
NOW:	119
Writer's Block:	121
Against Time:	122
Stomach Aches:	124
...	126

FOREWORD

We are living in a time where social media and television rule the minds of society. Where the next best thing is just a scroll away, and love is just another four-letter word. *Solitude is Company, Love is a Crowd* is an insightful journey into the mind and heart of one lover. A story told from and through the eyes of Andre D. Woods. His writings will captivate you as they take you on the quest of love, heartbreak, lust, pleasure and pain.
I have the great honor of calling Woods my best friend. As his close, personal friend, I have been around for much of what you are about to read, and have watched as this epic body of work came to life. These are his innermost thoughts. My hope for you is that you are able to find solace and inspiration and discover that you are not alone, that others feel and or have felt the same joys and losses as you.

    This prevailing poetic masterpiece tells the story of how imperfect LOVE really is. This is not a collection of your mother's "roses are red, violets are blue" poems. These are the blunt, in your face, fucked up truths of our hearts and minds. Andre D. Woods has taken the time to open his heart and allow it to flow through his pen and the ink that has bled onto the pages you are about to read will take you on a journey through the peaks and valleys of the rocky terrain that is love. Woods, much like a master of linguistic alchemy, has a command of the language and an ability to transform words into works of art that is unrivaled.

    Read *Solitude is Company, Love is a Crowd* as it is

written— a story of the rollercoaster of emotion in Andre D. Woods' whirlwind love life— or search out specific passages that ring true to you and your current situation. Are you alone? Are you in love? Are you in... lust? Have you loved and lost? If any of these questions ring true to you, then you've lived and that's what this book is about— life. So turn off the TV, put your phone on silent and enjoy with an open mind and heart.

 — James R. Shipp Jr.
  Model/Actor, Designer, Entrepreneur & CEO of
  ShippShape Consulting in Los Angeles, CA.

Solitude Is Company
Love Is a Crowd

Andre D. Woods

PHASE 1:

A Loan

A LOAN:

Shadows, whiskey, the sound of the city's infinite cry, and hundreds of crumbled pieces of paper resting beneath my pinewood desk. That is all I had left of her graceful wretched soul. The aftershock of love's presence is what we pay for. The value of nostalgia can only be exchanged for dignity, for pride, for peace of mind, for sanity. Happiness has expensive taste, as it is sweetly bitter at the bottom of every glass... as it is eye watering when consumed... as it is pain, once gone.

Temporary it was, to have her heart. As this empty bedroom of mine pays me back in the city's weeping over a silent room, and the stars shine just enough to keep me awake, I am all out of whatever kept oblivion in my possession with only...

shadows, whiskey and the sound of the city's infinite cry...

As I was only loaning my happiness... to be alone... Love... is only a loan, I tell ya.

MOON LOVERS:

We only met under the moon, her and I. We both agreed the sun would never understand our chaos. A glass of whiskey or her choice of wine, with some music, and we would dance with the shadows and fuck until the stars played hide and seek with every moan that jumped out of my window. Until we felt the walls of my room blush in humiliation. We knew how to love in the most temporary of ways. It was our avenue of sparing each other the indifference. But after all was said and done, we would just lie there. As our sweat mixed among the sheets of my bed and formed a chemistry we fought to avoid... Then for a split second, we daydreamed in the dark.

The sun was inevitable, I tell ya... Still, she always left before sunrise, although it never really made a difference.

Nobody can dodge   loneliness.

Rain Drops:

It was a summer evening and the rain poured without purpose. It was much too hot to wear my hoodie and much too wet to sit in a t-shirt. One of those lose-lose type of days as I waited for my ex, or my girlfriend, or my friend that I screw from time-to-time, to pick me up from work. There was a girl, mid 30's with a cigarette, a briefcase and an umbrella. She offered me cover from the rain....

"No, thank you", I replied, even though I needed it.

She continued, "Who are you kidding?" As she stepped to the side and our shoulders touched. I could smell her body spray and hint of cigarette smoke when she got closer. She had a bittersweet scent to her soul, as she tried to cage the pain away with cheap perfume... It was refreshing in the worst ways.

"It is moments like this..." she began to rant....

"... When I get to watch the rain drop from the sky, attempting to focus on one drop at a time... but I always fail to see it through. There's always a good ol' distraction."

At this point I was a little lost but my ride was not here and unfortunately the rain stops for no one.

As she continued... "There's always a good ol' distraction. I should have stood under the rain like you..."

"Andre!" I stated.

"Pleased to meet you Andre! I should have stood under the rain like you, and waited for that one drop to fall and land right on my forehead. But instead I lost track of him, staring into the drops that fell around me."
She paused and took a sigh as if she were going to cry. I could see a volcano erupt inside her eyes.
"Here, you can have this shit!" as she handed me her umbrella and walked away, eyes watering like the sidewalk, with only her cigarette and briefcase rolling behind her.
I left the umbrella, as my ride pulled up to the curb. I hopped in without a drop of rain, just me and my distraction, as I watched the rain fall from the passenger window.

Liquor Infused:

A bottle of whiskey and thoughts of her are the ingredients for disaster. The two are much alike in the most beautifully deranged ways.

This glass of misleading truth is so good to me after every sip. Brings memories to life and kicks the shit out of reality. But once I wake up tomorrow, it will be gone, vacant, empty to it's uselessness, and it will fucking hurt… Just like her.

She floods my mental every time I stare through the bottom of a shot glass. It's the chaos I need, just to keep her around a little longer.

Party Girl:

She drank until she had to vomit. With blind eyes she threw up every drink the bartender served her. I stood behind and watched her regrets flush down the toilet. I wasn't really good at that type of stuff– grab the hair to stop it from going into the shitter and say things I didn't mean to comfort her. It was all I really knew, and it worked. She cried tears while she kneeled to the porcelain omega, and somewhere inside the weep of a belligerent woman I heard heartbreak within each gasp. Goddamn it she used to be in love, and even the sweetest girls rot in the consequences of trust. It was like watching a flower ascend from the filthiest of soils. Tomorrow she may bloom from all this nonsense.

A garden of shit we live on, but every now and then a rose will grow, or a drunken young woman will vomit out her ex boyfriend's soul along with the other poisonous wastes from her stomach.

GONE GENIUS:

I fell for a stranger once before. I watched her pop a pill and fall in love with every human that looked into her vision. I realized it was not the high she chased, it was the ability to fall in love and never feel heartbroken, it was the numbness from the lows.

She was a genius, the girl with dilated pupils. The music played, we locked eyes, and she walked away. As I stood there, shattered in my sobriety, envious of her escape.

"Goddamn it, love is just a gateway drug..."

EYES TELL LIES:

> *I almost loved someone who loved someone else, that didn't love that someone back...*

She was easy on the eyes, this girl, with very little ease in her own. She had pupils surrounded by red trails from dragging herself along the pavement of her memory lane, and under those eyes were two body bags. As she cried tears in hopes to drain her leftover passion which could not be resurrected. An unfortunate case of essence, she was. I wanted to fall in love with her.

But goddamn it the tired eyes tell secrets, I tell ya, and I just put eye drops in mine.

I almost loved someone who loved someone else, that didn't love that someone back...

She was easy on the eyes, this girl... and that is all she really was.

Morning Ritual:

Ring! Ring! Ring!

"Snooze for fuck's sake," I scream at the top of my mind. Sleep is much better when a naked goddess is shaking you by the shoulders, interrupting your dreams. But what is a man with only a wallet full of words to do when the city swallows a swan and spits out a crow painted in gold? I never needed an alarm with her around... She wasn't much of a sleeper and I wasn't much of a morning person, as the sun and I didn't have much in common but the desire of her skin complexion. She was a walking bottle of honey Jack I tell ya, and I drank her soul until I blacked out in her mind and here I am...

With a bed three times my size, six pillows, a hangover and an alarm clock that annoys me more than my ex.

"Who needs work, when there is nothing to go home to?"

As I give myself a moment to loathe.

RING! RING! RING!

As I wake the fuck up,

scratch my scalp

and invite the city

to swallow me.

Just as she did...

BODY OF TIME:

An hourglass figure, she had, with love like quick sand. The only time I had her in the palm of my hand was when her hair hugged my lifelines and wrapped around my grip, she felt much like forever. That was when I had full control. But when it was all said and done and my back wore the footprints of her fingernails, and my neck stood stained by her lips, she would just slip away and fall between the crevasses of my fingers. As if we had never touched. The hands of time were the only hands to grab and keep her attention.

An hourglass figure, she had, with a love like quick sand

BAND-AID BOY:

You were wounded and I was just a fucking Band-Aid, covering the pain, just there to stop the bleeding from your broken yesterdays, to aid the healing process. After the cut was gone you ripped me off quickly and disposed of our temporary bliss. All I had left to show were bloodstains from all the mistakes someone else had made.
If only time waited for you to use me once you healed. I would have caressed your scars until they were classified as beauty marks. But goddamn it writers are only used for reminders. To add a little dose of hope, and then the assholes just shoot it back down again... until another Band-Aid goes to waste.

LOVE SICK:

I have drunk three of those little cups of cough syrup... Sick as a dog.

As my forehead burns like the bridges we once created, and the hot chills that followed your touch intrude my skin behind cold sweats.

These covers still reek of your scent... and I think the pillows have saved your moan within the cases, as I can hear your pleasure in my sleepless evenings.

My heart used to pound in double time for you. It is funny how my brain has taken the responsibility.

The flu and your absence are much too alike...

I hope this is only the flu.

I heard when you fight sleep you begin to hallucinate.

The

more

my fever

goes down,

the closer

I feel you

next

to me.

I knew you'd come around...

Losing It:

Lose your keys,

your wallet,

your phone,

your purse,

your fucking parking validation

and you lose your mind scavenging to replace the steps; a dance of insanity, it is.

...As I did she...

We never really know how we misplace the things we need until it is too late to find... or until someone else finds them....

I have yet to grasp my mental.

All in a Night's Work:

I didn't know her but she asked me to love her for the night… We took shots of whiskey and each shot became a celebration of another year. She explained her pain and as she spoke, I could see unwelcoming memories pacing in the hallways of her heart's abode, and as the gloom of the story rose darker, I became more intrigued by this stranger that is now the love of my hour. Five shots in and I could visualize the past five years of her life. I was mad enough to believe I knew her.

I could not tell if I was drunk, or if I had fallen in love. Either way, I'll regret it tomorrow.

Falling in and out of love… all in a night's work.

Cheers to You:

I drink,

and I drink,

and I drink...

to drown your existence out of my imagination... wash you away from my stream of thoughts with waterfalls from whiskey rivers and the flood of unforgiving memories flowing inside my mental...

But this bottle, it favors your silhouette, and after a while it becomes the closest thing I have to your heart and I hold it even after it sits in emptiness, even when it stops changing me.

I drink,

not to escape you, but to resurrect the intoxicating moments... of you.

*"Maybe we are not repeatedly falling in love.
We are just hopping from one pain, to a better one."*

ROSE:

When I met her I knew

I would never fully

have her.

It made it

easier to

consume the

disappointment.

She spoke hope into

thin air as I inhaled poisonous promises.

Who was I kidding?

True love is extinct, along with all my foolish hopes.

What was I thinking, speaking of expectations?

She found the

closest distance

before the

touch and when

I reached like a

fool she disappeared

into my yesterdays.

I'll never look at a rose the same, as they are only beauty

picked from the root and used to temporarily fill a void...

until it vanishes, into a memory.

SOUL SWITCH:

Are you asleep, old lover?

If you are, am I stained upon the lenses of your imagination?

Are you awake, old lover?

If you are, am I polluted within each inhale of every breath?

Have we accidentally swapped our sanity within the mess we've made?

As I see your eyes within every human I look into.

As every thought of the future fades into a memory of your existence.

As the bottom of every glass ends with an aftertaste of the saliva from your tongue.

Are you here old lover, or are you gone?

As your presence still haunts me in your absence.

I am lost.

Am I there, old lover? Have you taken me with you?

Stood a Chance:

You always resisted the feeling, like the clouds blocking sunrays to drown inside the deepest, darkest parts of the ocean... Love started ripples, heartbreak created tsunamis and after the disaster, victims laid along dry shores covered in hourglass sand and stains from your lipstick...
Nobody's ever survived your chaos... but nobody's ever stood a chance from the start.

As you have always anticipated an end to it all.

Dreamless Evenings:

A night without a dream

without a nightmare...

When one o'clock in the morning transforms into four in the morning and the moon begins to envy the sun. Sometimes I think she sucked the dignity right out of my mouth during our last kiss. Her tongue was a thief, I tell ya. That's when it happens— we open ourselves...

our souls, our mouths, her legs, our arms...

and we surrender with hospitality until the happiness wears its welcome, until comfort gets greedy, until one walks away with all hope and the other just watches the moon envy the sun... *without dreams, desperate enough to chase nightmares... haunted by a sleepless reality.*

Until you hope for it to happen... all over again.

PRETTY BIG CITY:

The problem lies within the nice looking people in this city. The faces are much too flawless nowadays. We have all found a way to easily hide the pain.

As the syringe pierces the skin and fills it with yesterday.
As the makeup shapeshifts the natural happiness of a smile.
As the filter erases the unique scar.

Beauty is a saturated industry, I tell ya.
As we all fear the disappointment of meeting someone and realizing they are not perfect.
How refreshing it will be, to see beauty and pain on one face.

Cold Summer:

Her heart embraces the warmth from those hot summer days and carries it into those cold winter nights... as if you were only made to love under blankets near the fireplaces with hot chocolate placed upon your lips... and then summer came back around and your love froze over, as your days are spent taking advantage of the sun with wintry intentions. Cold-hearted, she was... Her lips blew snowflakes for kisses and spoke of warm love within the sub-zero temperatures of her intentions, and although I began to get frostbite from time to time, I was still mad enough to ice skate straight into a broken heart. I knew her blood was chilled, but goddamn it, her soul would

be thirst-quenching if someone

could just melt her heart.

"Average Joe"

– Words from Jane:

"I knew a man once before; Joe was his name. He sucked qualities out of women, infused them together and used them in attempt to fill a void in his heart that was created by fear of his yesterdays. He hid under a flawless exoskeleton of pride like armor on a knight, absent of ever stepping foot on a battlefield. A joker in disguise, he was. He searched for all of the qualities missing from his previous lovers and used them as pieces to build his ideal being... but at the end of it all, when his masterpiece was complete, he only crafted a sculpture of himself with a hole on the left side of his chest holding a hand without a face. None of those women ever had his heart. They were only scraps, to help him build his flaw.

Oh, Joe, as I have met him everywhere."

"Average Jane"

– Words from Joe:

"Did it hurt? When you fell from the sky and realized this world is a fucked up rock we all have vandalized. You were an angel until you allowed these humans to clip the soul of your wings and sell them to a false dream.

So I ask to remind you, if it hurt, when you fell from heaven? Because now you are a dime a dozen, a penny in a car cup holder. You have forgotten where you came from. I have lost you somewhere in a tomorrow you should have never been promised.

Oh, Jane, as you are a shiny pawn in a Hollywood chess match."

THE FEELS:

Numb, she was... with skin like a cemetery. Every chill, every goose bump died with the last son of a bitch who found the perfect touch. But goddamn it, the touch is only half the battle.

If only my tongue could resurrect the hair that rose from the stimulation. I'd lick her life and speak her love back into existence.

Yesterday's Junky:

She was a fucking junky for the past. I've caught her snorting lines made from the dust of a broken hourglass and filling old tears into syringes before she injected her veins with every reason not to fall in love again. She would doze off into yesterday and wake up in cold sweats as she'd fiend for another fix. Just sprinting from tomorrow.

She hated the drugs but not more than she cringed at the thought of ever falling in love, all over again.

Talking to Myself:

I have loved you painfully, as if there weren't any other option but to love you. At times I wonder if I am just another fool with tunnel vision, a lonely man with a typewriter and a bottle of whiskey. But even if this rotten heart of mine were blindfolded I would still gravitate towards the thought of you...

Wherever you are...

Post-traumatic love:

Her purse holds weapons of mass destruction... with tear gas-infused perfume for any man that gets close. A blood red lipstick case hiding the bullet that awaits the first victim who goes for the kiss, and mixes gunpowder with her blush to remind herself of the soldier she is every time she puts on her makeup.

She used to believe in love until her heart went missing in action. Getting done up was a hobby, an avenue of beauty. But when a cut is made, a scar forms. Now every time she looks into the mirror to get ready... she gets ready... for war.

PHASE 2:

Love: Oblivion at Its Finest

Love: Oblivion at Its Finest

Sitting in a silent room and my attention span seems to fail me once again. Reading is a drag at times… but I always have an ear for the city's weeping…

The paramedics ring through the streets, but only for a pretty penny… death can really put the next man in debt, I tell ya. These days it is much too expensive to be unfortunate…

The cars honk behind cars that honk behind cars and somewhere at the finish line of the domino effect an insurance agent is pickpocketing a man with only a box of cigarettes, a missing bumper and liability insurance.
  – **Just listening to life happen.**

My apartment building walls might as well be made of hemp paper. Next door there is a crying child and a young couple fighting to hurdle over the loudness of each other's argument. They mentioned custody, yet the subject cries alone, with only a blanket and something to gaze at on the ceiling… and one day some school counselor will give them a pat on the back and encourage them to keep their head high.

– Just listening to life happen.

I remember being a child and hearing the pill bottles shake like an instrument to a junkie's favorite song. It came from my mother and father's room. I didn't read much then either. Their footsteps from the bed to the cabinet began to slow down as their song began to fade away... and once the music was over, and the sound was empty, and the instrument no longer rattled to the rhythm of their likings... the weeping began as the bottle sat topless in vacancy... just as the city... the sound of Los Angeles... does this to me at times, sidetracks my mind...

But she is here now... It is time for oblivion to run its course... Her presence is like earplugs from reality... I can hear her footsteps slow down at the door... as her keys begin to shake at the lock of the knob... Her approach is a rhythm of my likings... something like my favorite song, I fear the day it fades.

– Listening to love happen Until the day Life does, as well.

THE GREATS:

...The eyes, they start a lot of shit, I tell ya.

That's how it all happened...

Our imaginations fucked for hours before we even got close enough to touch. We got deep, far before the penetration. My tongue touched her core before I ever got to taste the center of her being. Her lips wrapped around my undivided attention between the five feet of space and she blew my mind. She knew how to turn the hands of time as if they were her very own. Distance was like a box-spring and we used it until it was devoured by desirability.

That's how it happens; it's best that way.

A good fuck is a good fuck, but The Greats stick around. They hold a craft, from practice. We practiced each other with space. She was one of the greatest, I tell ya... She mastered the craft of me.

NOURISHING PAIN:

I knew I was screwed, when she kissed and bit her deepest fears into my neck. All her reasons to push away traveled down the chills of my backbone and I had to live with it.
That is how it works. The acceptance— it must travel in the blood and even if it hurts it feeds you life.
You live with it— the baggage. But you must do it willingly and show the worth of it all.
With a smile.
With a kiss.
With a moan.
With enough madness to welcome the pain.
"Keep me alive with all that kills you."

       ...I told her.

Been There Done That:

I've held hands with a woman as we spied on the sun creeping behind the ocean. Long walks on the beach followed by nights spent counting the stars… and I've slept with the nymphomaniac that awakened the filthy skeletons and came out for a good screw every now and then…
But she… she took the monsters, skeletons and beasts and convinced them to dance with the gentlemen, chivalrous and saints within my soul. Her love hosted a shit show party inside the venue of my existence. She pinpointed my madness and every piece of me celebrated for her.

Unreal:

We conquered a whole bottle of wine and her fingertips drove the lifelines of my palms in infinitude, driving under the influence of momentary nostalgia and even if the touch was temporary, I was convinced I had forever sitting in the palm of my hand.
The reality of it didn't fucking matter. It didn't even exist.

BEST OF BOTH WORLDS:

The dead weight of our unclothed bodies against each other kept us alive... We loved through irony, I tell ya. Her lips would tease my ears as she inhaled without a word. A bite on the lobe spoke imagery far beyond words... I slowly inhaled as she consumed my fantasies, from the passion in my vessel to the filth at the bottom of my twisted mind. Her soul accepted my entirety.

She became a material of every utopia my imagination had ever fabricated.

A mixture of reality and fantasy, she was.

A Love/Fear Poem:

Allow me to escape your dreams while I rest upon the floor of your rock bottom. I will lay there with your sorrows and inject my veins with the tears you keep boiling inside those volcanic emotions. I will live with your tribulations pumping through my heart as it filters into the purist gesture to feed your soul. Your pain drives my madness to love you.
Every kiss I have for you comes from your worst fears, my dear.

Fun and Games:

A recreational human, you were supposed to be...

A fill for my bottomless cup of temptation...
> *As the high slumbers inside the mind for an evening.*
> *As candy is for the child.*
> *As the sweat is for the bed sheets until it dries.*

I left my tongue inside you long enough to love the moment but never more as I fled the aftertaste of you...

A bad habit, you became...
> *As the needle is for the shaken arm.*
> *As candy is for the adult.*
> *As your scent is to my pillow case.*
> *As our memories are to the tip of my tongue.*

As permanence is to the temporary intentions.

Instincts:

We kissed and your lips shook as if volcanoes were erupting inside the abandoned islands of your heart… Your fingertips grazed me and then pulled back like ocean wave endings at the peek of a shore. My eyes were the moon and every time they shined, yours would drop like the sun, neglecting a contact that could change the universe forever.

I could tell you hadn't loved in a while.

Your fear of it has become second nature.

A GREAT FUCK:

"Come here," I said...

As she stood there, unclothed, washing her hands in my bathroom sink... the water ran as I dazed and wrote thoughts of my desires along the outline of her silhouette... An ideal moment, it was; the air conditioner blew right when the sex was over with her sweat seeping into my pores, staining my soul... and there she was, hands clean walking directly toward me. She painted the perfect picture within the shadows of my dark room. The moonlight fought to touch her in ways I did.

These are the moments of truth,

when the nails are done playing music on the vinyl of the skin, and the filthy words echo inside your memory while the climax sits on the tip of your sigh of relaxation.

These are the moments we realize there is more to the blood rushes before a good fuck...

... Because once we both came... we stayed.

"Come here," I said, as she walked back into my bed.

Filthy Gentlemen:

Always be a gentleman.

Open doors, offer your jacket, look her in the eyes, and place the chair behind her before sitting... all that's good stuff.

But every now and then you must dance on the the fine line she awaits.

Get a full hand of the behind until your fingertips graze the unexpected, whisper filth into her imagination at family gatherings, place the tongue where it does not belong and give it a new home.

... But always remain a gentleman, a detail you mustn't forget.

Touch her in all ways non-physical.

Giver her intellectual orgasms in multiples and allow temptation to drip from her ears. Go down on her thoughts and taste her perception.

Learn her soul and she will fill the void of your filthiest imaginations.

Never start with the hands.

I bet the raindrops race

T

O

F

A

L

L

on your

existence.

ALL BUT SLOW:

Love you slowly?

That is not in my nature.

There is nothing slow about my heartbeat in your presence... it swing dances to the melody of your voice...

There is nothing slow about the thoughts in my mind. As they all race to beat the constant thought of you, failing tremendously.

There is nothing slow about my stomach. As it turns at world speed from your slightest touch.

These goose bumps rise and fall, giving standing ovations to each sense you trigger in midst of my weakness for you, and these senses are ignited rapidly. Slow and love are incompatible... impossible, I tell ya. Control is lost when love is found, and love will only be found when the uncontrolled is in our acceptance. I can only love you, the way I love you.

... All but slowly.

MIDNIGHT:

Staring outside the window of a dark sky...

As the moon slowly illuminates this shadow of a world. Just as she loved me, a love soft enough to maintain the beat of my heart; yet alive, I did not feel. Every thought of her ascended as a star, in hopes of landing on the moon. As the quiet breeze grazes my skin, I then felt her touch; chills rose above my tattoos as the hairs on the back of my neck danced slowly with my goose bumps, but only to the music of her fingertips.

Oh the nostalgia of midnight, the only time between today and tomorrow, between the beginning and the end. The only time she allowed me to love her. If only the moon knew how to love beside the sun....

Staring outside the window of a dark sky, staring straight into her eyes.

Universal Attraction:

I've seen the way the sun reflects against her skin as if she were the surface of the ocean under the sunset during the magic hour.

How raindrops procrastinate to evaporate from her body in hopes to seep into her soul...

The moon lives inside the glare in her eyes and every day she shares it with the sky and brightens the world's dark room we call night.

The universe favors people like her and she compliments the universe.

Fuck Buddies:

We were supposed to be fuck buddies.

I knew I was screwed... when I started to notice the little things.

We would go at it until our pleasure became an exercise, as if sex were a competition.

I watched a drop of sweat travel down her lower back.

She had an arch that could scare a tsunami away from the shore and goddamn it, I drowned in the way we made love.

We were supposed to be fuck buddies.

But she was much more than the expectation.

Staring Problem:

"What are you staring at?"

She always caught me within the tunnel vision of her pupils. She had a way with taking in all that I was thinking, and storing it in a dark place, and she didn't even know it. I stared at her without reason, free of logic.

> **As the homeless man strolling, does the sidewalk.**
> **As the stargazer, does the moon.**
> **As the madman, does the white room.**
> **As the artist, does the world.**
> **As the life-sentenced inmate, does the gated window.**
> **As loved ones, do the sunset.**
> **As the insomniac, does a dream.**
> **Without boundary,**
> **without hope,**
> **without freedom,**
> **without answers.**

I stared at her only for the utter and complete oblivion from all that surrounded me.

As a human, does love.

As I replied...

"Huh?"

Layers:

She stripped for me...

First she removed the pain from over her shoulders.

Unbuttoned the fear.

Pulled down and

stepped out of the

insecurities.

I watched her lay back, slip her past from beneath her

existence and throw it all behind her.

She spread her heart wide open for me.

As I placed her passion along the tip of my tongue until she

invited me to fall

deep inside

her love.

TOAST:

When she loves you, get drunk.

Drink until the world no longer matters.

If you black out and remember those three words, take the rope of love and hang yourself with it. Fall in it.

For the life she lives includes you and your death will no longer matter. Become reborn with a life of her.

Drink, my friend.

Drink.

PHASE 3:

Crowded by Love

Crowded by Love:

As fucked up as it sounds, some of us are made to love the monsters of the world... with the audacity to rip the ugliest characteristics out of a human by giving them the utmost beautiful things. By inhaling sunsets and exhaling a sky full of stars in a world wretched enough to ever give a shit about you.

Some of us carry enough strength to fall apart just to show someone how beastly their soul really is.

As fucked up as it sounds, some of us are only expenses for another human's growth, and as much as it ties your stomach into a million knots...

...you did a good deed, you shattered human.

BUSINESS IS BOOMING:

Our souls are made from shredded
operating agreements of love.
Puzzled back together with a lousy
business plan our minds have created, I tell ya.

The strategy of smoky hearts
cloud the oxygen and fog the fear of falling.

The cost of beauty is a pretty fucking penny
in a poor industry of fools.

"A booming business, it is."

The future of this city haunts my reality
in small episodes, as I sit back and watch...
I see non-disclosure agreements
signed before spoken vows
and relationships molded into sponsorship programs...

Love is becoming a job...
and soon we will be unemployed due to our poor judgment.

TWISTED ATTRACTION:

She is wretchedness wrapped in beauty. Every touch was only meant to stain my mind after her absence...

Her tongue carves symbols of lust into the walls of my soul...

She is the hell that fell from heaven, a blessing dipped in sin, an angel stripped of its wings, holy water mixed with venom.

I can hear my last breath within her whisper. I can taste death in her saliva. I can feel the dead end in her kiss.

She is wretchedness wrapped in beauty, a reason humans pray for forgiveness, the giver of all temptation, the taker of all hope.

She is absence. She was beauty.

She is wretchedness wrapped around me.

SMOKERS AND LOVERS:

I blew smoke in the air, got high and watched it disappear before my eyes.

Just as you did...

I don't even smoke and you were never the type to love...

As we both have stepped outside of ourselves for a feeling that never seems to last.

Houdini:

Magical– this is the feeling we all described it to be. Well, you couldn't have described it any better, as you continuously pulled my hopes out of a hat and made it all disappear. You drew me as your KING of hearts and quickly turned me into a joker. Left my dignity on display, cut it in half and showcased my foolishness through the beauty of your deceit.

You are a magician, an illusion of love putting on a show for your troubled ego.

So magical it is, to play the fool.

HALF EMPTY IS ENOUGH:

"*I love you,*" I said, and at that moment I felt like a performer exposing my passion in the empty auditorium of her heart.

It was a love I had worked on for quite a while, day in and day out.

She was the only member in the audience and when it was all said and done, she did not applaud my love with reciprocation.

There was only silence.

The blank sound of disconnection, a performer's biggest fear.

What can one expect? It does not happen at the same time. The first to say the words is usually the one that walks away with a half-empty cup.

As I sit here, typing... with only me and a small sip of whiskey left to finish me off.

Shadow:

I loved her like her shadow.

It understood the parts of her unreachable to the sun.

A place the world fails to recognize… and in the dark it wraps her spirit and comforts her in places that these humans will never learn to appreciate.

Her shadow loves her so effortlessly.

But she only lived for the sun.

Mind Within Matter:

I am far too much of an over-thinker, so I've been told. So tell me, how did my mind feel when your shaken legs rested upon my shoulders... all of my thoughts, from memories to hope, invading your soul. Your submission was like a vacation, old lover, and freeing my mind within you was all so bittersweet. So tell me, how did it feel? To lay back and take in all you would never understand?

SIMPLY COMPLEX:

The little things, that's all she ever wanted.

I never understood it until now.

Usually the way life works— you don't see the big picture until it's gone.

She desired small signs of appreciation, as I was much too busy trying to make billboards of my love, looking away from the present until I had it all figured out. But we never really figure these things out.

She vanished within yesterday like the small things do... If only I kept doing the small things....

Simplicity has become so complex.

Good Gal:

She was petite, easy to pick up but very hard to let go. Not very driven by sex but could take the wheel of any man's sex drive.

Long hair.

Short-tempered.

She loved on paper, with structure.

Her heart beats along a timeline.

We would sit in passion; I would release my entirety but she always had a little piece of her soul hiding behind her back.

My hands would attempt to travel the world upon her skin as her hands patrolled the southern end of her universe.

She sold me sex with her aura, I tell ya, but never with the physicality of her existence. Patience was her middle name and she never gave me her last. She was good at what she did, but even better at what she didn't do.

The type of lover that never got too close, as she avoided the bad she anticipated after it all.

She was a good gal, but I know once she goes bad, she will be even better.

...a good gal, but only until someone is good enough to handle the other half.

Out of Mind:

We only fell in love when our eyes shared the scene. Our skin felt the touch and our lungs tag-teamed the air... as a fiend does the fix and the moon does the belligerent; drugs are only drugs when you aren't high, and drunk is only drunk when you are sober.

The clock ticked in our favor when we were together, I tell ya. But distance always seemed to cause us amnesia, as space flooded all that we remembered and time began to give us a hangover.

Out of sight, out of love, it seemed.

SMART PHONES, DUMB LOVE:

Hold my heart like your phone and panic from my misplacing.

Lay me beside your bed as you sleep and I will remain to wake you and start your day, my dear.

Look proudly into the front camera of my pupils and force your self-beauty into the storage of my memory.

I can sing your favorite song, assure you never get lost and be there to distract you from this world.

Love me like your smart phone, it is my only hope of keeping you here with me.

World vs. I:

I loved her before the world did, I tell ya.

When the mascara smeared around the pain in her pupils.

When the dark wrapped its arms around her loneliness.

When her dreams hid from her sleep and reality overstayed its welcome after midnight.

I drove through the red trails of her bloodshot eyes just to find out she only lived for the world. For the littered attention wasted along the city streets. For the lights blinding the conscious and the music staining the character.

I loved her far before the world did, I tell ya, but the world is all she ever wanted.

She is created with all the impossibilities in my mind.

She is too good to be true.

She is love.

She is fallacy.

She is a created impossibility in my mind.

The Getaway:

"*I'm sorry.*" (walks away)

She wore her best outfit.

Her face made up lightly, just how I liked it. *I hated when she caked her makeup.*

Hair was done as if she'd just left the salon.

Heels clicked along the sidewalk with a dress that allowed the ass to wave me goodbye one last time.

The scent stuck around, it was her way of letting go slowly, *such a kind gesture.*

It was all premeditated: the love, the sex, the laughter, the smile, the hate, the indifference, the end.

A spoken love without a soul is a crime, I tell ya.

An apology before a mistake is only a planned escape.

PHASE 4:

Accompanied by Solitude

Accompanied by Solitude:

There is a type of love that is far worse than any dark room, from any heartbreak or loss of trust.
An agony beyond loneliness.
A plain love, one absent from happiness and empty of pain.
Where the laughter hides inside the shadows
and the anger sleeps under the bed frames,
just waiting for the stale silence to overshadow their existence.
Until they disappear.
Where the hands lock much more than the eyes,
and the lips touch far more than the tongues.
Where sleep is easy and dreams are forgotten in the morning.

There is a type of love that will make you feel normal.
That will make you forget you are alive.

I never really knew much about myself. The best way to research your soul is inside the darkest of rooms. Being blinded from everything physically surrounding me is an avenue to living inside my own being. A closed eye once taught me a majority of what we see is only a distraction from the never-ending journey of who we are.

I remember sitting over the highest point of the city, where the couples steal beauty from scenic views and sew them into their love. I sat there, eyes closed, neglecting the skyline, ignoring the beauty that fed from my pupils. Finding myself sitting at the highest point of the universe, looking down at my puny existence. I stared into the sky on the cloudiest day of the year and saw more light than the sun could ever grant me.

Alone is free,

without direction

and nothing around me,

when all has lost me... I am found.

TATTOOS AND I:

"*Let's fuck!*" she whispered...

As she placed her lips beside my right ear, close enough to hear her inhale before each sentence...

"*I want to kiss your tattoos until they begin to fade away...*"

It was a poetic line, to say the least. I could have taken her to my apartment and introduced her to every skeleton in my closet. Maybe let her dance with the monsters of my imagination and sing to the shadows. But somewhere trapped under the sangria that raced from her words and the hint of smoke scented from her hair, I pinpointed the sweet innocence of her perfume... somewhere before she waltzed into this bar she sprayed that elegant collarbone of hers, stared into the mirror and embraced the purity of her solitude.

...I thought to myself, *"How the fuck could I ignore that...?"* As I replied, "Go home, my dear, my tattoos will always be here..." as I closed the taxi door...

FORGET:

Cover the pain with unstopped time, my dear.

Be busy.

Live in the gym and lift the weight of every memory off the shoulders which I kissed in shadowed rooms.

Be busy.

Go to class without distraction and exercise the mind I once used as a treadmill.

Be busy.

Watch what you eat, and create a routine within your twenty-four hours.

Be busy, old lover. Clothe the pain with time until the only hands you hold tick back in your favor and mine fade into the background.

Disappear:

The closest thing to immortality, love.

But it, too, fades like the fog as the sun opens its eyes slowly towards the day.

So when your heart begins to beat in normality, and the butterflies in your stomach begin to stop giving a flying fuck, or the oxygen we share begins to only feel like air, let go slowly...

Like swallowed gum traveling through the body, or a child learning to ride a bike,

let go slowly...

Like an empty syringe rolling from the fingers of a dozing addict, and a dream tiptoeing away from a shitty reality,

let your soul evaporate from my lungs, as if you were never even there.

BREAK THE HEART:

Pull the chair from beneath.

Watch tears fall with a straight face.

Dodge thrown objects. Dodge phone calls. Dodge quality time.

Fall asleep on the wrong side of the bed and wake up on the wrong side.

Look into the phone more than the eyes.

Break the heart.

Keep speaking of love when it's left the building.

Settle.

Let comfort be the excuse.

Spend time without quality. Make calls without want.

Allow history to control the future until the present is forgotten.

...Sometimes you have to be the bad guy and break the heart. As it is inevitable anyways.

Safe in Pain:

She never really let me get too close, I tell ya… and you don't notice these things until it's all said and done.

When the knife sits perfectly inside your chest as if it were planned and the leftovers of her existence stain the air like gunpowder.

She knew her heart was below zero…

A cold piece of work, she is. Far from the touch yet she can make you feel close.

She is safe this way. The intentions of these men are no different than the acts of a civil war, and she holds a sniper over it all.

So far from her heart, but close enough to shoot yours down.

She feels safe, without love.

BARS AND DREAMS:

If only I found her twenty minutes sooner.

Before the four shots of vodka slithered

through her bloodstream, racing to

drown her conscious, and the blank stare

in her eyes was painted with the

curiosities of "what if?" as opposed

to "what now?". Before her fears

lay down and split their legs

for temptation.

If only I found her with the doubt

of the world laying across her shoulders.

I would have tried to prove the reality she ran from wrong.

Writer's Ink:

I used to think the ink from my pen was made of the mascara that would fall down her face along with the tears. I attempted to write pieces that targeted my right from her wrong and in the end, it would always seem to flip on me. As if karma put a curse on my words and added a sharp edge to the end of every one of my sentences. I began to stab myself with my own thoughts; a writer's suicide is what I call it.

It felt so good to touch this paper with my mind, but in the end I realized I could never lie to myself.

COFFEE SHOPS:

There is somebody for everything, I tell ya.

Every corner store holds the unfortunate sitting outside.

Every bar has a broken human.

Every park carries a free spirit.

Every classroom has a failure and successor.

Every coffee shop has a me.

..and every me... has yet to be found.

Sooner or later.

SHHHH:

There is a silence that sings to you in the shadows. It sings a painful song with a raspy voice by a cigarette smoker of forty-plus years, but it's a song that understands you, a silence that keeps you company. Sometimes the sunrays burn you with too much of what is good for you and the voice of reason sits inside the whisper of your crowded mind. People come with a lot of bullshit at times, more like all the time, too much of a sugarcoat will rot your spirit. But silence— it is authentic. Even when it pierces through your soul, it will tattoo your character with learned lessons. There is nobody to lie to, nobody to explain to... just you. There is a silence we all deserve to have, pain and all.

Comfort

is

only

a

fuel

for

fear...

Those

who

sit

in

the

same

place

too

long

are only running from change.

COMPANY:

It is so empty when the lights are on. As I sit in this room alone...

In the dark the used space from the light becomes full of all the thoughts I keep hidden underneath the staircase of my sanity. It is a state of mind the sun would never understand. Solitude and darkness have been there for me long before the sun. I am in my element in this room of a pitch-black audience, with only me.

The more humans around me, the lonelier I become.

Solitude is company, the best kind.

Mr. Know It All:

"*What the hell do you know about love*?" she screamed before she threw her right high heel.

The makeup from her eyes slithered down her cheek like wax from a candle.

"*Actions speak louder than words!*" Balancing on one foot, stumbling to grab her other high heel.

I knew she wanted a reaction. As I was not consumed enough to give her one, but I studied her like material.

I could see the wick burning in her pupils. There was a fire in her soul and it could demolish a village of non-believers. She fought wars within her frustration to get my love to fight back, even if it was against her... All she wanted was a good fight.

She got in arm's reach. The hands shook and I saw chaos in her love, a natural disaster, an uncontrolled beauty as her fists became defibrillators against my chest. Yet this apathetic heart of mine would only beat in normality.

"*What the hell do you know about love?*" With her head on my chest, tears smeared against my t-shirt.

I could have written all that I observed and explained, but actions speak louder than words.

"Nothing, my dear." I replied... as I had nothing to show for it.

Laws:

If these hearts of ours had laws, I bet they would ban time for eternity. Clocks would be handless and hourglasses would fill to the top without any empty space to tell us when to start and stop...

...And we, well, we would have never feared the use of something that means absolutely nothing. We would have been much more valuable...

       ...than time.

Voids:

There is a void.

It will remain vacant, unfilled.

Time will not do the trick. There are only distractions.

We are made of these things, voids, scars... that never go away.

We just go on; until someone is powerful enough to dig a new void worth suffering for.

But there is happiness within the process, which is what measures the value. The good times are like a shovel, and the more you share the nostalgia, the deeper the hole.

But there is happiness, I can assure you that much.

ANOTHER DAY, ANOTHER DRIVE:

Yesterday, I drove to work and saw a young boy kicking rocks, two businessmen shook hands, a woman with a nice ass jogging at a still light, a couple of college kids riding their cruisers and a homeless man telling the wind a wise story.

A day in hell it was, when the universe really bends you over and fucks with your dignity. That night my bottle of whiskey was emptier than a rich man's mansion on a Monday afternoon. My ex came and got the stuff she left in my apartment, looking flawless, but not for a second into my eyes... did I mention the whiskey being gone? I stubbed my toe on the goddamn couch and some punk-ass kids broke into my car... Still no whiskey.

Today, another drive to work and the young boy still kicked rocks, the businessmen shook hands again, the woman with the yoga pants jogged the neighborhood like always, the college students rode bikes and the homeless told another wise story.

Life goes on, I tell ya.

Perspective:

If she only could have viewed the world though my eyes. If she could see the dark seas of her very own soul and the land of her broken essence.

I never wished to have the beauty visible to the stranger: the ass, the hair, the eyes, the lips, the smile. That is all much too simple. I wanted to backpack the existence she hid from and bring forth the essence of her entirety. The parts of her that she hid from the sun...the parts she hid from herself.

If only she could have viewed the world through my eyes. She probably still, would not be here.

Non-Social Media:

I look into my phone to see these messages:

"Why can't you text me back?"

"You can post on social media but you can't return my phone calls?"

"I saw you tagged in your friend's photo last night! Where were you?"

All of the questions she asked me quite often. Very logical questions, I must admit.

The world is built for reality these days. Everyone is far too involved in the motion of another human. Technology is not made for love, I tell ya. Every question she asked me led to the justice of her argument, every statement was poisoned by reason. The truth does not always set us free, I tell ya. The truth should not always be told. There is no space within the distance, just more reason to get a little closer. With all that was said and done I found myself in a lose-lose situation. Quite frankly it would have never worked from the start...

As I did not reply, and we never spoke again... but we still see each other every day as I scroll down the screen with my right thumb.

"There are too many fish in the sea to be pissing in someone else's pond."

NOW:

It may be the key to love: time… When time is on your side its hands will massage your presence until the future and the past are put to rest.

It may be the key to hate: time… when time is not on your side, its hands will stab you with every second you turn away from its effort.

It may be the key to time: *now*. As we mustn't lose track of its existence.

"Walk towards the sun with a fucking purpose. As if every human you've ever loved is dragging along the edge of your shadow."

Writer's Block:

For fuck's sake, I have lit fires with my soul fighting to love you with every fucking molecule within me.
Burned poems of your love and threw them into blood rivers that stream within my veins, but goddamn it, people like me aren't meant for those things. This ink would not bleed if I could love you whole-heartedly and you wouldn't have loved me if you did not doubt me. It's the risk, the feeling of danger... we chase it for no fucking reason, I tell ya. Logic has no business with these types of situation.

AGAINST TIME:

These are the hours of truth.

Without control.

Where some humans dream peacefully, some rest in nightmares, but they sleep. Others poison themselves to unconsciousness and the rest fight to escape reality. There is no stopping it... The sane mind can only contain it for so long. Time can only be avoided momentarily. The poison can only jade your influence until you reach the limit. Busy can only dance with the imprisoned thoughts for so many songs.

Until it happens: truth...

Like Pandora's box.
Like a secret amongst children.
Like a caged animal.
Like a deranged celebrity.
Like a heart... Like a mind.
Like this very moment.

Like you.

STOMACH ACHES:

I had a long drive home from another day at work, and in the middle of it all, it hit me. The Mexican food I ate on my lunch break crept up on me and made it to the top of the list of my priorities; *much like she did*. My stomach spoke and I listened, but there wasn't much I could do about it, *as it wasn't the right time*. I could have pulled over and used the restroom in the gas station, but I was better off shitting in the middle of the street and I did not have much time to stop and be told that I couldn't go.

It's crazy how it works— *how something can just take full control of your divided attention and consume you. When all you can think about is the one feeling, good or bad.* These types of things control your mental and create tunnel vision, I tell ya.

I finally made it home, rushed to the bathroom and took a seat.

Suddenly the ease massaged my mental as I took a deep breath and let it all go. At the moment I realized *she was only temporary, a priority in time...*

It seems as if sitting on this toilet is the best type of meditation for me these days. The only time you can lock yourself in a room and not worry about someone wanting to come in and invade your privacy. *She was so important to me at one point in time.* But like memories, she too must flush, until some other shit comes around.

...

We all want to fucking know these days.

Scavenging for the answers, for these razor-edged sentences to fill the limitless void...

But goddamn, it never does. We are all just questions in the flesh and the only answer is that feeling, the feeling right before death, during the last breath...

Knowing too much will drive you mad, I tell ya... It will ruin the unknowing beauty of that very last feeling.

Cheating life, we are all trying to do, as we take shortcuts with our souls.

Love in question, and the answer will live inside the feeling. The feeling, sometimes, may best be proven when it is all said and done. Solitude is the best type of company, when love does not fulfill you. As death is the only answer to the questions in life, which we will never seem to understand.

"I try to turn every single experience and emotion; whether it is with friends, family or strangers and transform them into a love story. We all have our own unique insight on life, which makes it nearly impossible for me to expect the reader to understand my chaotic direction. But we all have experienced love, heartbreak and hate; it is our emotions broken down to its simplest form, a universal language. There is something about never fully understanding the heart, that makes it easy for us to embrace all it has to offer, pain and pleasure.... and I am quite fond of that..."

Andre D. Woods
Instagram: @A.D.Woods
Twitter: @ADWoodswrites
www.AndreDwoods.com

CPSIA information can be obtained at www.ICGtesting.com
Printed in the USA
BVOW02s0347230316

441426BV00024BA/181/P

9 781682 411728